Contents

		Page no.
Chapter 1	Introduction	3
Chapter 2	Understanding Your Emotional Landscape	6
Chapter 3	Nurturing Your Emotional Wellbeing	11
Chapter 4	Fostering Connection and Support	23
Chapter 5	Embracing Meditation, Mindfulness, and Gratitude	28
Chapter 6	Embracing Change and Growth	35
Chapter 7	Conclusion	39
Appendix 1	About the Author and Kaleidoscope	40
Appendix 2	What if page	43
Appendix 3	Connection Table	47

2

Chapter 1 Introduction

Welcome to "Embrace: A Journey to Emotional Wellbeing," a Book designed to guide you on a path towards nurturing your emotional health and finding greater contentment in life. In these pages, you'll discover valuable insights, practical tips, and gentle encouragement to help you navigate the ups and downs of your emotional landscape.

Life is a beautiful yet complex tapestry of experiences, filled with moments of joy, challenges, triumphs, and setbacks. At the heart of this journey lies our emotional wellbeing, which influences how we perceive and respond to the world around us. Just as we tend to our physical health through diet and exercise, it's essential to cultivate our emotional resilience and inner peace.

In this Book, we'll explore various aspects of emotional wellbeing, including self-awareness, self-care, resilience, and relationships. You'll learn how to embrace your emotions with kindness and compassion, develop healthy coping mechanisms, and foster a deeper sense of connection with yourself and others.

So, take a deep breath, open your heart, and embark on this journey with an open mind. Remember, you're not alone on this path. Let's walk hand in hand towards a more fulfilling and emotionally balanced life.

Chapter 1 Introduction reflection

What aspect of your mental health do you require the most help with?

If you received this help, what would your life be like one year from now?

On a scale of 1 – 10, one being leave me alone I am perfectly fine the way I am and 10 being change me now, how much do you want to change?

Chapter 2 Understanding Your Emotional Landscape

Emotions are the colourful palette of our inner world, painting the canvas of our experiences with shades of joy, sadness, anger, fear, and love. In this chapter, we'll delve into the depths of our emotional landscape, exploring the nuances of different emotions and the role they play in our lives.

- **The Power of Self-Awareness**: Self-awareness is the cornerstone of emotional intelligence, allowing us to recognize and understand our feelings, thoughts, and behaviours. Through mindfulness practices and introspection, we can deepen our self-awareness and cultivate greater emotional resilience.

- **Embracing All Emotions**: Each emotion serves a purpose, offering valuable insights into our needs, desires, and boundaries. By welcoming all emotions without judgment, we can develop a healthier relationship with ourselves and others.

- **Honouring Your Authentic Self**: Embracing your authenticity means honouring your true thoughts, feelings, and values, even when they may not align with societal expectations. By embracing your uniqueness, you empower yourself to live a more fulfilling and meaningful life.

The Power of Self-Awareness: scanning your body from head to toe and toe to head asking yourself "what am I feeling and where am I feeling it?". You need to do this several times a day to ensure that your emotions don't run away with you, and you suddenly find yourself losing your temper or bursting into tears and you are not aware of where that came from, which usually leaves you feeling embarrassed or ashamed or frustrated. Scanning our bodies many times a day and dealing with the emotions as soon as you identify them allows you to deal with the emotions as they arise. You may not be able to identify the emotion initially, especially if you are not used to checking in with yourself, therefore, naming the sensations can help enormously. Is what you are feeling sharp or soft, near or far, spikey or smooth, heavy or light, dull or bright, does it have a sound, a colour, a smell, a taste? Your answer to these questions can help you to identify if what you are feeling is pleasant, unpleasant, or neutral. Really in the beginning that is all we need to know.

Embracing All Emotions: Once you have completed your scan and identified whether what you are feeling is pleasant, unpleasant, or neutral you can then ask yourself what is this emotion showing me? What it shows you usually falls into one of three categories. Things you can control i.e. your boundaries, your self-care, whether you respond or react, your thoughts. Things you have partial control over i.e., relationships, behaviours of people you are with. Things you have no control over i.e., weather, other people's health, war, politics, violence; but even with these you can have a little control in your own part of the world or your attitude to them or by writing letters to those that do have influence or control over these things.

If the emotion falls into the unpleasant and can control section, I recommend taking a piece of paper drawing a line down the middle. Take five minutes to write down on one side of the piece of paper all the unpleasant feelings, thoughts, concerns, or worries, I label this 'negative what if's' however, please pick a word that works for you. In the other column, which I label 'positive what if's', write down all the ways this could be different – usually the direct opposite of what is in the 'negative' column! If you do this in a book, make sure the negative column is on the outside of the page, then you can tear it out and you are left with a book with a lot of half pages but full of positive emotions, thoughts, and ideas.

Honouring Your Authentic Self: I believe depression is a need for deep rest, and it comes about because we have been playing a part for too long. Usually, the part we are playing is who other people expect us to be. The dutiful child, the loving partner, the doting parent, the conscientious employee. Your soul might be crying out to dance, to wild swim, to horse ride, to lie on a beach, to rebel, to run your own business, to be free. When we honour these desires, we can feel less depressed, more in control and calmer. When was the last time you explored your values, your own true thoughts on matters, or your own true feelings about something?

Chapter 2 Understanding your emotional landscape reflection

Power of self-awareness

Drop your attention into your body, scan your body head to toe and toe to head. What are you feeling and where are you feeling it? Was it spikey or smooth, near or far, large or small, heavy or light, bright or dull, did it have a taste, smell, sound, colour? Was it pleasant, unpleasant or neutral?

Embracing all emotions:

What is this emotion showing you? Is this something within your control, partial control or something you have no control over whatsoever?

See appendix 2 for example of the positive/ negative pages.

Honouring your authentic self:

Is there a way to honour your true authentic self that would help ease the unpleasant emotions?

Chapter 3 Nurturing Your Emotional Wellbeing

Just as a garden requires tender care and nourishment to flourish, so too does our emotional wellbeing. In this chapter, we'll explore practical strategies for nurturing your emotional health and cultivating a greater sense of inner peace.

- **Practicing Self-Care**: Self-care is not selfish; it's an essential act of self-love and compassion. Whether it's taking a bubble bath, going for a walk-in nature, or indulging in a favourite hobby, prioritize activities that replenish your spirit and nourish your soul.

- **Cultivating Resilience**: Resilience is the ability to bounce back from adversity with grace and strength. By reframing challenges as opportunities for growth, practicing gratitude, and seeking support when needed, you can cultivate greater resilience in the face of life's ups and downs.

- **Setting Boundaries**: Boundaries protect our emotional wellbeing, allowing us to honour our needs and protect our energy. Learn to set firm yet compassionate boundaries in your relationships and daily interactions, empowering yourself to prioritize self-care and authenticity.

Practicing Self-Care: If you were on an aeroplane and the oxygen mask came down and you had a small child with you, whose mask would you fit first – I hope you said yours. If not, here is why you should: if you pass out due to a lack of oxygen you and the child are now vulnerable and a burden on the flight crew who should be concentrating on helping other vulnerable passengers and trying to fix whatever is wrong with the plane. If you put your mask on first, you can then fit the child's mask keeping you both safe. Self-care is not selfish, you cannot pour from an empty cup, self-care is essential. But it also looks quite different for different people, it may be 5 minutes with a cup of tea, a warm bath – alone before bed, eating properly, exercising, scented candles, and drinking more water. For others it may be getting out of bed, having a shower, brushing teeth and hair, eating properly, exercising, hydrating properly. Self-care is not self-indulgence; it is vital for our health and wellbeing no matter what our circumstances.

There are five pillars of life. Physical, Social, Mental, Spiritual and Emotional.

1. Physical caring includes sleep, massage or self-massage, eating, staying active and taking care of your health.

Sleep is an essential part of selfcare. Chronic lack of sleep can lead to obesity, diabetes, and heart disease. This could be a whole book in itself. Try to go to bed and rise at the same time each day. Create a routine that signals to your brain that it is time for sleep. Ensure you environment is conducive to sleep. Reduce screen time before bed. Keep your bed purely for sleeping and intimate moments.

Massage or Self-massage is so beneficial to us. Humans need to be touched. When we are touched, we release oxytocin – the cuddle hormone which helps boost our immune systems. Touch reduces stress, calms our heart rate and blood pressure. When we are alone and can't be touched by others, self-massage can help us to raise our own oxytocin levels and boost our own immune systems.

Eating. You should be eating at least five portions of fruit and vegetables a day. Drinking at least eight glasses of water a day.

Health. Attend your appointments. Listen to your body when it whispers, and it will not have to scream. Reach out for help when you need it.

Staying Active. We should all be getting at least 150 minutes of exercise a week. However, this may look very different depending on ability and capacity. For some this exercise might be running, aerobics, Pilates, Gym work for others it might be armchair activities like armchair aerobics or armchair Tai Chi. For another set of people or on other days it might be NEAT (Non-Exercise Aerobic Thermogenesis) activities brushing floors, vacuuming, running around after children, walk about if you have an active job like nursing on a hospital ward.

2. Social self-care. Socialising and connecting with others is important for our well-being, meeting with friends to vent or have a laugh. Sometimes this is not easy. We can also help ourselves with our social self-care through our work or volunteering. The chat

around the water cooler in work can help our social self-care. Volunteering reduces the risk of depression, gives a sense of purpose and we can learn new skills, it helps us to stay physically and mentally active, may reduce stress levels, may help us to live longer and helps us to meet others and find new friends (of course all of this depends on the type and nature of the volunteering work we are undertaking) but in general helping and caring for others gives us a hit of serotonin and dopamine.

3. Mental self-care, in this instance we are talking about our ability to think, analyse and remember. We can stimulate and help our mental health with puzzles, sudoku, jigsaws, learning a new language etc, these all create new neural pathways and help to ward off Alzheimer's and dementia. Challenging our thinking patterns is also incredibly useful. If we notice we are thinking the same things over and over again and these thoughts are not helpful, we can observe them and see if we can change them by asking powerful questions – firstly something like, "isn't that interesting that I think…..", then maybe "what is this thought trying to show me or teach me?" Keep learning about yourself and how your mind works.

4. Spiritual self-care. Spirituality is believing in something bigger or beyond yourself. It can be a religion or a holistic belief in people's connection to each other and the universe. People who practice either a religion or spirituality are generally healthier. You can enjoy prayer or meditation, attend a service or ritual. Asking deep questions about topics.

Deepening connections with other people.
Demonstrating compassion and empathy.
Experience happiness beyond material objects.
Finding meaning and purpose in life.

5. Emotional self-care. It's important to have strong coping mechanisms for the times when we are angry, anxious, or sad. This can be things like the anchoring exercise where we remember a time of great happiness and anchor that emotion to ourselves. Meditating to deepen our resilience zone so that these feelings don't impact us as much. Breathing to enable us to gain control in those stressful times and understand that these are biological responses. Redirecting our thoughts by using our sense to pick our colours in a room or hear what else we can hear, or feel the chair beneath us, or notice what we can smell. Having and increasing our attitude of gratitude, this focuses our attention on the things we have rather than the lack. Staying active as a way of increasing our self-care and our resilience by increasing good hormones and experiencing natural highs. Emotional Freedom Technique (EFT Tapping) enables us to identify the emotions, feelings or sensations we are feeling, identifying how we want to feel and, if done correctly, takes the emotional charge out of a situation or memory allowing us to feel more at peace, calm and balanced.

Cultivating Resilience: Each of us has a resilience zone. The place in which we can cope with whatever is going on in our lives. Occasionally things happen that take us out of this zone. Practising our wellbeing tools can help to broaden our zone so that we cope better with life's turbulence. Wellbeing tools such as breath work, meditation, anchoring happy memories, redirecting our thoughts, grounding, EFT Tapping, mindfulness, gratitude, caring. All these tools when practiced often can help cultivate our resilience, our bounce back ability, because when we use these tools, we do not get blown off course or knocked so far out of our zone as often.

Setting Boundaries: Self-care is sometimes the hard choice. Setting boundaries for ourselves and others can be difficult especially in the beginning. The people who protest the most about your new boundaries are usually the people you needed the boundaries for the most. There are three types of boundaries: rigid, loose, and flexible.

We usually have a main style, but we can change given certain circumstances. For example, our main style might be flexible but when we are with people, we distrust our boundaries may become rigid, or when we are with people, we really trust our boundaries can become loose.

People with rigid boundaries usually keep other people out, keep them at a distance and help avoid intimacy. Rigid boundaries may be a result of a person having been hurt and wanting to withdraw from intimacy to avoid being hurt again.

People with loose boundaries usually let too many people know all their business, they let people get too close and give too much of themselves away, they can take on too much as they have difficulty saying no.

People with flexible boundaries usually have healthier boundaries and are more balanced, they know when and how to say no, but also when and how to say yes. People with flexible boundaries are also able to hear no without offence.

Chapter 3 Reflection

Practical self-care:

Are you getting enough sleep? If not, what is going on and how can you improve this situation? Where can you get help with this?

Do you go for massages, reflexology or anything like that? If not, can you give yourself a massage?

Do you eat at least five portions of fruit and vegetables a day? If not, why not? How can you increase the amount of fruit and vegetables you are eating? Can you make some swaps?

Are you drinking an appropriate amount of water for you a day? If not, why not and how can you achieve this? Can you make some swaps?

Do you go to the GP for a physical examination at least once a year? If not, why not?

Do you get 150 minutes of exercise a week? If not, why not? How can you increase this amount?

Social self-care:

Do you work or volunteer? Do you make time during the day to socialise with people either in work or in your volunteer role?

Do you socialise with family and / or friends? How often? Is that enough? If not, how can you increase the amount of time?

Mental (intellectual) self-care:

Do you do puzzles – jigsaws, mathematic puzzles, word puzzles or language puzzles? If not, why not? What needs to happen for you do do this for your mental health?

Are you learning a new skill? A musical instrument or a language?

Spiritual self-care:

Do you believe in something bigger than you? An entity, a belief system, a community? How connected are you to this?

Emotional (mental) self-care:

Do you have any anchors? Can you describe your anchors? If you do have anchors, can you increase the number of anchors you have?

Do you meditate? What is your favourite time of meditation? If not, why not? What do you need to help you start?

How often do you practice any breathing exercises? Ideally you should practice breathing for three rounds, twice a day. What is your favourite type of breathwork?

Redirect- look around the room how many colours can you see? What noises can you hear? Are there any smells? Are the smells pleasant, unpleasant, or neutral? What textures can you feel? Is there a texture you prefer? What do you taste?

Cultivating resilience:

Practising all the wellbeing tools above will help to cultivate your resilience. Can you choose at least one of the tools above that you will practice until it becomes second nature and then pick another tool etc.

Setting Boundaries:

Do you need to set boundaries? Are these boundaries for yourself or for others? If for others use these sentences to help get your message across: -

"When you do {insert behaviour} _____ I feel {insert emotion} _____. If you keep doing this, I will have to {insert consequence} _____. In future I would prefer if you would {insert how you would prefer to be spoken to or treated} _____. "

Chapter 4 Fostering Connection and Support

Human beings are social creatures, wired for connection and belonging. In this chapter, we'll explore the importance of nurturing supportive relationships and fostering a sense of community.

- **Connections:** build connections around you, with your family, friends, colleagues, neighbours. At home, in work, school, or in local community settings. Building these connections will support and enrich you every day.

- **Practicing Empathy and Compassion**: Empathy is the ability to understand and share the feelings of others, while compassion is the desire to alleviate their suffering. By practicing empathy and compassion in your interactions, you can foster deeper connections and cultivate a more compassionate world.

- **Seeking Support**: Asking for help is a sign of strength, not weakness. Whether you're struggling with emotional challenges, navigating a life transition, or simply need a listening ear, don't hesitate to reach out to trusted friends, family members, or mental health professionals.

Connections: Loneliness is bad for your health. Whilst building quality connections with deep and meaningful conversations is one goal, even just saying hello to someone on your daily walk or in the shop can help you and them enormously. We never know someone else's circumstances and for all you know the person you spoke to may not have spoken to anyone else that day. We build connections by taking the time to put ourselves out there. By going to see our family and friends. By attending community groups, my recommendation here is ask yourself what you love to do – crafting, singing, dancing, chatting over a cuppa – then go find a group that does that. If you're really stuck your local council may know some groups in your area or ask in your local library.

Practicing Empathy and Compassion: a bit like boundaries this can feel very uncomfortable to begin with but the more you practice the easier it will get. When you think someone is 'attention seeking' change this in your mind to 'connection seeking' and think about how you can help them to make better connections. Instead of judging a person for the choices they are making, ask yourself why they might be making those choices, put yourself in their shoes, what might have happened in their life to bring them to that place where they are making those choices.

Seeking Support: there is plenty of help there if you need it and you know where to look. If you are in Northern Ireland the Health and Social Care Trusts have a Directory of Services to help improve mental health and wellbeing https://www.publichealth.hscni.net/publications/directory-services-help-improve-mental-health-and-emotional-wellbeing. The Kaleidoscope Facebook page has helpline numbers on a pinned featured post at the top of the page www.facebook.com/kaleidoscopevcn You can reach out to me at Kaleidoscope or to other professionals or to family members or friends. Although this make us feel uncomfortable as we can believe it makes us vulnerable it actually takes a lot of strength to be vulnerable.

Chapter 4 Fostering Connection and Support Reflection

Connection:

Make a list of all your connections? Then note how often you connect with each individual? Is this enough for you? Is it enough for them? This may mean having a meaningful, slightly uncomfortable, vulnerable conversation with some of your circle to establish whether the amount of time is enough or not.

Then

How do you connect with people? Is this the most appropriate way for you? For them? This may need a conversation with them to establish why certain methods of connecting work better than others for each individual.

See Appendix 3 for a useful table.

Practicing Empathy and compassion:

Who do you feel in your life are the attention seekers? Can you remember the last time they displayed this behaviour? Can you now view that behaviour as connection seeking? If yes, how do you now feel about the person? The behaviour? And about yourself?

Seeking Support:

What kind of support do you need? Could you receive this support from family and/or friends? Of maybe a support group of people with similar issues? Or do you need specialist support?

Chapter 5 Embracing Meditation, Mindfulness and Gratitude

Meditation is focused concentration, mindfulness is the art of being present in the moment, while gratitude is the practice of acknowledging and appreciating the blessings in our lives. In this chapter, we'll explore how cultivating meditation, mindfulness and gratitude can enhance your emotional wellbeing and bring greater joy and fulfilment.

- **Meditation:** focusing on our breathing, or a piece of gentle music, or someone's voice, or a chant brings a sense of calm, relaxation and balance which can restore emotional wellbeing.

- **Mindfulness**: The present moment is where life unfolds, free from the burdens of the past and worries about the future. By practicing mindfulness meditation, deep breathing, or simply savouring the sights and sounds around you, you can cultivate greater presence and inner peace.

- **Cultivating Gratitude**: Gratitude is a powerful antidote to negativity, helping us shift our focus from what's lacking to what's abundant in our lives. Start a daily gratitude practice by keeping a gratitude journal, expressing appreciation to loved ones, or simply taking a moment to count all the things you can be thankful for.

Meditation: an ancient practice that is now practiced all over the world. Science has proven that meditation can lower blood pressure, reduce anxiety, decrease pain, ease symptoms of depression, improve sleep, and increase our ability to focus. There are different types of meditation and people should find the practice which works best for them. Start with short meditation two to three minutes per day and build up ideally to ten to fifteen minutes twice a day.

These are the six most popular practices:

1. Focused meditation: focus on your breath, or a noise, or staring at a candle flame (safely). This type of meditation does what it says increases our ability to focus. The guided meditations on my You Tube Channel fall into this category as you are concentrating on my voice www.youtube.com/@kaleidoscopevcn6758
2. Mindfulness meditation: Whilst sitting in silence if we have a thought, feeling or sensation we name it silently to ourselves. Do not be cross or upset with yourself, be pleased that you are noticing your thoughts.
3. Spiritual meditation: done in silence and is about seeking a deeper connection to God, the universe, spirit – whatever your belief system.
4. Movement meditation: walking in the woods, yoga, qigong, running, swimming, dancing or just walking forward a few steps and then back a few steps really noticing which bit of your foot is in contact with the floor.
5. Mantra meditation: according to quantum physics everything is energy and energy

vibrates, each sound has a vibration that relates to a feeling or a specific part of the body. Examples of mantras are 'Om', 'I am that I am', 'Om Namah Shivaya', 'So Hum', 'I am enough'.
6. Progressive Muscle Relaxation: clenching and releasing different muscle groups in the body and then tightening the whole body and releasing to induce deep relaxation.

Mindfulness: being aware and being fully present in the moment. A great mindfulness practice that can be done in the car when driving – whilst still concentrating on the road – first connect with your breath, just the action of breathing in and out, then try to deepen it a little and then notice how your feet feel on the floor or pedal, how does the steering wheel feel in your hand, are you fully supported by the chair and is your head sitting near the head arrest.

In work we can do the same thing (even in a meeting if we start to feel out of balance). Connect with your breath, your natural breathing pattern just notice it, then try to breathe a little deeper, how does your back feel against the chair, how do your legs feel in the seat of the chair, how do your feet feel on the floor, if you can and it is appropriate to do so lay your hand flat on the desk and feel how solid it is to the touch. The feeling of the support of your chair and the floor can also sometimes be known as grounding. Grounding can also be connecting with mother earth through bare feet on or in sand, soil, or grass. I would highly recommend taking time to sit with your feet in the grass or taking a walk barefoot on the beach it will help you to reenergize. Grounding stabilises bio-electrical circuitry and harmonises biological rhythms it is all to do with the electricity because the earth produces 7.83 Hz EM field (The Schumann resonance) and this helps bring our bodies back into balance. Lots of small studies show grounding increases healing abilities much in the same way meditation does: decrease in fatigue, lower pain levels, improve mood, sleep better, reduce blood pressure.

There are plenty of free resources on the internet, everything from 5 minutes guided meditations through to 5 hours music meditations. Explore for yourself and find what you like. Some days it will be one kind and another it may be something else, depending on what you need. Please remember this is a practice, start with shorter meditations and build up to longer, as said earlier, ideally 15 minutes twice a day.

Gratitude: warm feeling of thankfulness. Gratitude enables us to appreciate what we have rather than focusing on what we lack. Thinking and or writing down at least three things we can be grateful for in the morning sets us up for a good day. Thinking and or writing down three things we can be grateful for last thing as night sets us up for a good night's sleep. In the beginning we may need some help because we are not used to noticing the things we can feel grateful for so here are a few examples: waking up, a roof over your head, a warm comfy bed, electricity, heating, hot and cold running water, our loved ones, friendship. Once we start practicing this twice a day regularly, we start to notice the things we can be grateful for during the day, green lights, parking spots, a delicious cup of coffee.

Chapter 5 Embracing Meditation, Mindfulness and Gratitude reflection

Meditation:

Before you attempt any meditation for the first time notice how you feel beforehand. Try out each of the meditation mentioned on page 16, notice how you feel afterwards. Some will make you feel relax and sleepy, these are the ones to do at bedtime. Others will make you feel relax and energised; these are the ones to do at the beginning of the day.

Rate each type

1. Focused
2. Mindfulness
3. Spiritual
4. Movement
5. Mantra
6. Progressive Muscle Relaxation

Mindfulness:

Before you start an activity notice how you feel.

Can you bring your full attention to any activity, even just for a few minutes to begin with? For example, doing the dishes, making the dinner, ironing, driving, writing, reading, eating. Whilst doing any of these activities notice how your feet feel on the floor, how whatever you are touching feels in your hand, can you feel your clothing touching your body – how does that feel?

Notice how you feel after these moments of mindfulness.

Cultivating Gratitude:

Find something small enough to put into your pocket, purse or wallet. Something like a small stone or glass bead. Hold it in your hand and think of something or someone you can be grateful for; this item is now your gratitude item/ stone. Every time you see or touch this item/ stone you ask yourself "What can I be grateful for right now?" sometimes you will need to really look and dig deep to find something, other times something will spring to mind immediately. The more you practice this skill the easier it becomes.

Chapter 6 Embracing Change and Growth

Change is the only constant in life, presenting us with opportunities for growth, transformation, and renewal. In this final chapter, we'll explore how to navigate life's inevitable changes with courage, resilience, and grace.

- **Embracing change**: Just as the seasons change, so too do the circumstances of our lives. Embrace the ebb and flow of life with an open heart, trusting in the wisdom of impermanence and the inherent potential for growth and renewal.

- **Cultivating Adaptability**: Adaptability is the key to thriving in an ever-changing world. Instead of resisting change, embrace it as an opportunity for learning, growth, and self-discovery. Remember, you are capable of weathering any storm that comes your way.

Embracing Change: remember the leaves lose their leaves once a year and the trees use those leaves as fertilizer. There are only three things in life that are guaranteed – death, taxes, and change. The speed of change is increasing, and it can be hard to keep up. However, when you are open to the idea of change and are willing to flow with the change it will be less disruptive. I believe that when life becomes very difficult and really uncomfortable it might be showing you that you are on the wrong road, and you may need to change.

Cultivating Adaptability: adaptability is your ability to adjust to the changes happening around you. We accomplish this by being responsive to new information, asking questions and doing research. Be part of the change, be open to suggestions, this may include stretching yourself which may be challenging so seek support. Keep learning, this will help you keep up with the changes and hopefully reduce the amount you need to stretch. Identify what is within your control, partial control or not in your control at all, and be proactive on the things that are in your control. Take the initiative, show that you can adapt to the changes. When we accept that nothing stays the same it gives us the freedom to look for new opportunities.

Chapter 6 Embracing Change and Growth reflection

Embracing change:

What changes have taken place in your life so far

Being weaned from milk to solid foods, transitioning from nappies to underwear, being at home with mum to going to creche or nursery to school to leaving home and becoming independent. Walking everywhere and taking buses to riding a bike and / or driving a car.

Cultivating Adaptability:

Think of some other changes that you have gone through, have they all been good or bad? Pleasant, unpleasant or neutral. What can you learn from each of these situations that you take into another situation? Maybe you can learn something from previous unpleasant situations that you can use in future situations? Is there something in the pleasant situations that you can use in future unpleasant situations?

Is there any one you know that has already been through this situation that you can ask questions or are their articles on the internet that you can read about this situation?

Chapter 7 Conclusion

Congratulations on completing your journey to emotional wellbeing! Remember, this is just the beginning of a lifelong adventure filled with growth, discovery, and transformation. As you continue to nurture your emotional health and cultivate greater self-awareness, resilience, and compassion, may you find joy, fulfilment, and inner peace in every moment. Embrace your authenticity, honour your emotions, and trust in the wisdom of your heart. You are worthy of love, happiness, and all the blessings life has to offer. So, go forth with courage and confidence, knowing that you have the power to create a life that truly reflects the beauty of your soul. Embrace your journey, embrace yourself, and embrace the incredible potential within you.

If you want to learn more about these wellbeing tools, please read the blogs on my website www.kaleidoscopevcn.co.uk

If you are stuck in any of these areas in your life, contact me for a free consultation
https://calendly.com/kaleidoscopevcn1/clarity-calls

Appendix 1

About the Author & Kaleidoscope:

My name is Valerie Crozier-Nicholl, a 50 something cancer survivor whose work took over her life!

Sometimes we reach a point in our life where we realise that something must change, or something will give. And that is exactly what happened to me.

Shortly after recovering from cancer the first time, I realised that my work had become all consuming. A job I once loved in the Public Sector overwhelmed me with so much stress that I no longer recognised the person I had become.

In one very clear moment I realised that I had to make a change.

Learning about resilience has been the foundation to help me create the life I want for myself. With the support of my loving husband and family, I took control of my life. Recognising that it is never too late to make the right choices to help me achieve my goals.

As I learnt all about resilience, I began to believe that everyone should have this information, these tools and be able to use them to help themselves, therefore, I started Kaleidoscope.

Kaleidoscope is an emotional wellbeing coaching company. We aim to help people go from stressed to calm using a range of modalities NLP, EFT tapping, Meditation, Breathing and Hypnotherapy for PTSD.

I chose the name Kaleidoscope as it refers to a collection of butterflies. There is nothing wrong with caterpillars but one day they decide they need to change; they create and enter a chrysalis. People imagine that during the process of metamorphosis the caterpillar grows wings. However, the caterpillar actually almost completely breaks down and then regrows. Using the newly grown wings to break out of the chrysalis strengthens the wings. The butterflies then rest, stretching the wings to let them dry, before flying away.

Moreover, a Kaleidoscope is a collection of broken glass pieced together to make beautiful patterns. I see my business as helping people put back all their broken pieces to create beautiful lives after going through a metamorphosis.

Appendix 2

Take 5 minutes to write all the negative thoughts. Then take a further 5 minutes to write all the positive thoughts. The most effective time to do this is within the last hour before going to bed. Photocopy this page as many times as you need.

Positive / happy / affirming What Ifs	Negative / unhappy / denying What ifs

When finished your list but out the negative/ unhappy / denying what if list and bin.

Appendix 2

Take 5 minutes to write all the negative thoughts. Then take a further 5 minutes to write all the positive thoughts. The most effective time to do this is within the last hour before going to bed. Photocopy this page as many times as you need.

| Positive / happy / affirming What Ifs | ✂ | Negative / unhappy / denying What ifs |

When finished your list but out the negative/ unhappy / denying what if list and bin.

Appendix 2

Take 5 minutes to write all the negative thoughts. Then take a further 5 minutes to write all the positive thoughts. The most effective time to do this is within the last hour before going to bed. Photocopy this page as many times as you need.

Positive / happy / affirming What Ifs	Negative / unhappy / denying What ifs

When finished your list but out the negative/ unhappy / denying what if list and bin.

Appendix 2

Take 5 minutes to write all the negative thoughts. Then take a further 5 minutes to write all the positive thoughts. The most effective time to do this is within the last hour before going to bed. Photocopy this page as many times as you need.

Positive / happy / affirming What Ifs	Negative / unhappy / denying What ifs

When finished your list but out the negative/ unhappy / denying what if list and bin.

Appendix 3

Connection table

Contact name	Where do they rank in your life 1 closest, 10 most distant	Where should they be in your life	How do you currently connect with them? Telephone call, text, what's app, social media, email, letter	How would they prefer for you to contact them?

Connection table continued

Contact name	Where do they rank in your life 1 closest, 10 most distant	Where should they be in your life	How do you currently connect with them? Telephone call, text, what's app, social media, email, letter	How would they prefer for you to contact them?

Printed in Great Britain
by Amazon